A PRIMER OF LEFT-HANDED EMBROIDERY

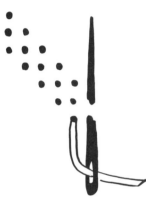

A PRIMER OF LEFT-HANDED EMBROIDERY

Carole Robbins Myers

CHARLES SCRIBNER'S SONS
NEW YORK

Library of Congress Cataloging in Publication

Myers, Carole Robbins.
    A primer of left-handed embroidery.

    Bibliography: p.
    1. Embroidery.   I. Title.
TT770.M9   746.4'4   73-1105
    ISBN 0-684-13841-7 (cloth)
    ISBN 0-684-15143-X (paper)

3 5 7 9 11 13 15 17 19 MD/C 20 18 16 14 12 10 8 6 4 2
1 3 5 7 9 11 13 15 17 19 M/P 20 18 16 14 12 10 8 6 4 2

Printed in the United States of America

CONTENTS

AUTHOR'S NOTE

This book started on a trip to northern Vancouver Island where I was given a Crazy-Quilt patchwork kimono. In the process of embroidering around the patches, I had to look up how to do many stitches that I couldn't remember. It was a lot of trouble translating them into left-handed instructions. Since I didn't want to have to work these through every time I used the stitches, I started making drawings of how to do each stitch left-handed. After a while it occurred to me that other left-handed people would find this useful. I thought of the pleasure that doing embroidery has been throughout my life and wanted all left-handed people to be able to enjoy the craft also.

I started the book with the intention of doing all the writing, drawings, and photography myself. It was a creative project in which I could have everything done just exactly the way I wanted. I was lucky to find Lydia Vickers Wunsch, a book illustrator and jacket designer, and had her do the more difficult drawings. She proved to be a tremendous help in really understanding the book and producing beautiful drawings. Another help was The Custom Darkroom who did a good job, carefully printing from my photographs nearly all the stitch pictures in the book. A final polish was given to the entire book by Elinor Parker of Scribners, and here it is! I hope you, the reader, will learn much and use what you learn to give you enjoyment and create beautiful things.

Carole R. Myers
Cambridge, Massachusetts
January 1974

INTRODUCTION

As a child I was fascinated by puzzles in which numbered dots were connected. Over and over I dutifully hunted for the next higher number to draw a connecting line from the last dot. Then, suddenly as if by magic, a picture appeared. It was always amazing to see that picture emerge from all those numbered dots.

Follow the dots has stayed with me, for when I attempt to describe the tying down of threads twisted and turned in a regular fashion to decorate a fabric, I conclude that the simplest way to communicate exactly how to embroider these stitches is to follow the dots. In this grown-up version of the game, you do not look for ever-increasing numbers but read the directions telling you where to place the needle into the fabric, where to bring it out, when it is to pass over a thread, and how to wrap the thread around the needle. If you follow these directions carefully, using the dots described for each stitch, you will very quickly be embroidering every one of these stitches—magically!

Every stitch has its own configuration of dots specifically designed for you to produce that stitch in the simplest way possible. These are called Guidemarks.

Watch an experienced embroiderer work, and notice how regular and perfect a row of stitches looks. Even if one stitch is a little lopsided, the next compensates so that the entire row looks good. Experienced needleworkers can easily do this because they have practiced these stitches over and over and have developed the "eye of an embroiderer." The "eye of an embroiderer" sees exactly where to place the needle into the fabric in order to get good-looking stitches. With the "eye of an embroiderer" one knows, when placing the needle into the fabric, exactly where it will come out. In short, the person has developed the ability to visualize the entire stitch, or row of stitches, before embroidering it.

How do you develop the "eye of an embroiderer"? This is definitely something that comes from practice. However, it is most important that you practice using a good model. Guidemarks will show you subtleties about the size, shape, and proportions within any stitch. Using Guidemarks you will be embroidering stitches that look expert. After some practice you will find you have learned enough to no longer need the Guidemarks.

The book is in two major parts: Part One, Things You Should Know Before You Start; Part Two, Stitches.

Part One will give you the background information so that you can follow the embroidery instructions. It will tell you most of what is necessary to know before learning these stitches.

Part two includes seven "family group" chapters of stitch instructions. Each chapter has the same plan, so you can pick up the book anywhere and understand the form of the instructions. In each of these groups the first stitch of the chapter is the basic stitch of that "family." All the stitches that follow that basic stich will be growing variations of that stitch. The sequence of stitches within each group is arranged so that where it is possible what is learned for one stitch forms the basis for doing the next stitch. For that reason it makes sense to go through the book sequentially, but this is not mandatory.

The instructions for each stitch are divided into three sections—Description, Guidemarks, and Procedure. A written Description of the stitch is accompanied by a photograph showing finished stitches and one in the process of being embroidered. If the stitch is generally done in rows, the description may be written describing it that way. Also included in this section is any additional information about the stitch that might be of interest or necessary to know before starting. The second section is Guidemarks. It is necessary to create guidemarks in order to follow the embroidery directions. This section tells how to draw the dots and lines for the Guidemarks for that stitch. There is also a drawing showing how the Guidemarks look. Procedure is the major section. This gives step-by-step directions for embroidering the stitch. Each step is accompanied by an illustration which shows how that step is done. By following each of these steps in sequence you will learn to embroider the stitches.

PART ONE

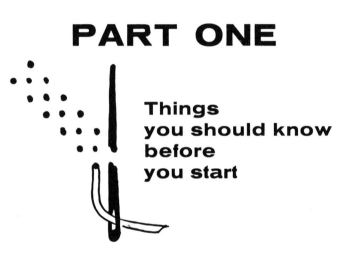

**Things
you should know
before
you start**

"On the Beach" by Hilda Kraus, Westport, Connecticut. Embroided Wall Hanging, wool on synthetic and cotton with beach shells; charcoal grey background; beige, brown, orange, cream wools. *Courtesy, R. Brooke, New York City. Photo: Yvette Klein*

1 ⬀ ABOUT THE BOOK AND LEFT-HANDED EMBROIDERY

This book is intended for both the experienced and the beginning left-handed needleworker to learn a variety of embroidery stitches.

Left-handed people know only too well that unless instructions are turned around to their mirror image they end up working in the most awkward fashion possible. Trying to mentally visualize embroidery instructions can be difficult. Trying to remember a great number of stitches, some of which are complicated, is clearly an impossibility.

From this book, with drawings and instructions set up especially for the left-handed, you can learn all the basic stitches of embroidery and many of their variations. Your knowledge of these stitches will give you the ability to follow the stamped patterns included in commercial kits or to use the stitches together with imagination to create your own designs. As you learn more and more stitches you will find that you can embroider more complex, varied, and intricate pieces. But even with only a few simple stitches you can create attractive embroidered pieces.

The instructions are easy to follow, and they teach the stitches completely from the left-handed perspective. The book begins with the simplest stitches; each subsequent stitch builds on what you have already learned. Its chapters start with a basic stitch and are followed by complications and variations on it. Every stitch has three sections: Description, Guidemarks, and Procedures. As part of the Description a photograph shows each stitch being done and what it looks like completed. Guidemarks are dots placed onto the embroidery fabric so that you can practice the stitch as the directions indicate. The Procedure section uses line drawings to illustrate the step-by-step instructions.

Experienced embroiderers have developed such a practiced eye that they know almost intuitively exactly where to place the needle for each aspect of a stitch. They visually measure equal distances between and within stitches in a row. For the beginner, using guidemarks will provide the structure needed to create regular stitches, embroider the stitch correctly, and help train your eye to see as well as the exprienced embroiderer. Soon you will find yourself experiencing the rhythm and flow of embroidering that make the craft enjoyable and relaxing.

The instructions in this book are precise, and if followed as closely as possible you will get a good-looking stitch; however, superfectionism is not required to create beautiful needlework. Variations and imperfections give a beauty to handmade items that you cannot get from those made by machine. In this age of ever-increasing mechanization the charm of the handmade is thought of as a positive asset.

You will notice that all the embroidery stitches are done with the needle going into the fabric from left to right and that vertical rows of stitches are always worked from the bottom up; these are the left-handed directions. You can get stitches that go down and up between two dots as one stitch if you use the following technique: place the needle into the fabric; then while still holding the hoop with the thumb and forefinger of your right hand, use your center finger from the back of the fabric to guide the needle point out at the next dot. When you pull the needle through, it will be from the front of the fabric using your left hand.

2  MATERIALS

For practicing stitches you will need

Fabric	Scissors
Thread	Ruler
Needles	Pencil
Embroidery Hoop	"Press-On" Dots

Fabric

A yard of a solid-color, loose-weave fabric should be enough. A linen or linenlike fabric is ideal. The weave should be loose enough to sew along one thread; this will help you keep the row of stitches straight.

Thread

The most familiar embroidery thread is six-strand cotton. For most work this is too thick, as it comes off the hank; separate it into at least two pieces of three strands each. I prefer a perle (pearl) French embroidery cotton. This is a double twisted thread with the look of silk. It does not need to be split and is used as it comes off the spool. Somehow, this thread seems to help my stitches slide together easily.

Needles

Standard embroidery needles are called "crewel" needles. A package with assorted sizes will be what you need. For certain stitches you will also need a "round-eyed sharp" needle.

Embroidery hoop

For the purpose of this book, which is to teach stitches, you'll need a small-size hoop, a wooden one four or six inches wide with a screw fastener is best. It will hold the fabric tight enough to prevent it from slipping and keep what you are working on clearly placed in front of you. Put the fabric on the smaller hoop, loosen the tension screw to make the larger hoop even larger, and fit it over the fabric. When it is in place all the way around, tighten the tension screw. The hoop is always held in your right hand. Experiment to see where holding the fabric will make your embroidering most comfortable. On the vertical stitches try holding the fabric slightly to the right.

Scissors

A small embroidery scissors is needed for cutting the thread. Embroidery scissors made especially for left-handed people with the blades reversed can be bought in good notions department.

Ruler

You can also buy left-handed rulers in art supply stores; the numbers begin at the right edge. You'll need a six-inch ruler marked in eighth-inch divisions.

Pencil

To mark the guidemarks on your fabric. One with a hard lead and a sharp point will help for clear markings.

"Press-On" Dots

These can be purchased by the sheet from the art-supply stores. The sheet contains dots of varying sizes. Choose the size you want, place the sheet over the penciled dots, and rub the dot into the fabric.

Two large manufacturers of "press-on" dots are Lettraset and Chartpak.

3 ⚕ SETTING-UP GUIDEMARKS

The instructions for learning each stitch are set up for you to follow guide-marks. It is important that you get these dots onto the fabric in exactly the spacing described before you start to learn the stitch.

To draw good guidemarks:

1. Lay fabric on a flat surface.

2. Place ruler on the fabric, trying to keep the edge along one particular thread.

3. Using a pencil with a sharp point, place it against the edge of the ruler and follow the instructions for dot placement given with each stitch. Be sure to measure accurately.

4. Place the "press-on" dots over the pencil dots and rub them onto the fabric. All lines and curves can be drawn onto the fabric with a sharp, dark pencil.

Thread and Needle Chart

THREAD	EMBROIDERY NEEDLE NUMBER
Pearl Cotton 5	crewel needle no. 5
Pearl Cotton 8	crewel needle no. 6
Stranded Cotton	
1 and 2 strands	crewel needle no. 8
3 strands	crewel needle no. 7
4 strands	crewel needle no. 6
6 strands	crewel needle no. 5

Detail of Crewel Bedspread. American, made by Elizabeth Linsley in Northford, Connecticut, before her marriage to Jonathan Tyler, December 1769. Partial set of bed hangings worked in varicolored wools. Width: 75 inches. Length: approx. 58½". *Courtesy, Historic Deerfield, Inc.*

PART TWO

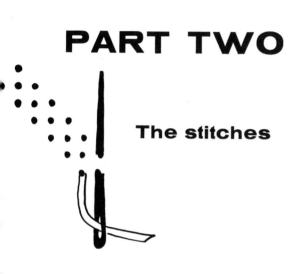

The stitches

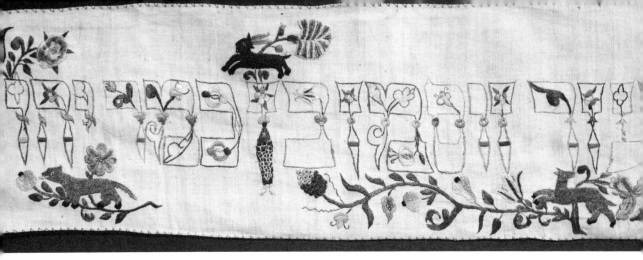

Torah Binder, Germany, 1731, linen. *The Israel Museum, Jerusalem. Photo: David Harris*

Gentleman's Cap. 18th century, embroidered night-cap. Chain stitch, red and green thread on white linen. Green and white tassel on top. *Courtesy, Historic Deerfield, Inc.*

1 STRAIGHT

Running Stitch

DESCRIPTION

The Running Stitch is a series of straight thread stitches with equal spaces between them. If you have done any sewing at all you are probably familiar with the Running Stitch, a series of dashes along the guideline. By sewing close rows of the Running Stitch you will create a textured effect. Another variation is to alternate the position of the stitches in adjacent rows. To start a new row turn the fabric around so that you are still sewing from left to right.

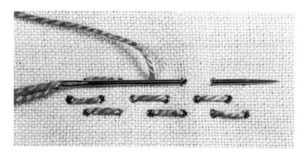

GUIDEMARKS

A horizontal line of dots.
The dots are a quarter inch apart.

· · · · · · · ·

PROCEDURE

1.   Holding the needle in your left hand, begin by pulling the knotted thread up through the leftmost dot.

2.   Place the needle into the fabric through the next dot to the right and bring it out one dot further to the right.

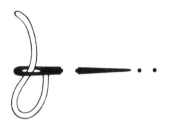

3.   Pull the needle through so that there is no slack thread, but not so tight that the fabric gathers in any way. Continue along the row with the needle going down and then up at the dot marks.

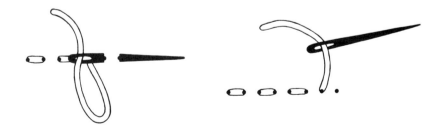

Weaving through rows of Running Stitch

Double the distance between stitches and embroider a row of Running Stitch. Using a thread of a contrasting color, start from the left end of the row of stitches bringing the needle under the stitch threads without going into the fabric. Alternate, going from above the stitch down, to going from below the stitch. This is called the *Wave Stitch*.

Triangle Stitch

DESCRIPTION

The Triangle Stitch is an equal-sided triangle with a split base. A row of these finds each triangle sitting atop the point of the previous one. The stitch is embroidered in three groups of steps. When embroidering the row you start at the bottom and work up the row doing the first half of the base, then down the row to the bottom creating a side, and finally all the way to the top again completing the stitch with the second half of the base and the last side.

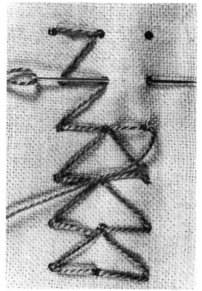

GUIDEMARKS

Three parallel vertical rows of dots.
The dots are a quarter inch apart.
The rows are a quarter inch apart.
The dots in the rows are opposite each other.

PROCEDURE

1.   Bring the thread up at the center bottom dot. Place the needle in at the left bottom dot and out at the center dot next above.

2.   Continue up the guidemarks forming the left half of the triangle's base. The needle goes in at the dot to the left of the thread and out at the center dot next above. At the top stitch ignore the left dot.

3. To create the diagonal that comprises one side of the triangle, work back down the row of straight stitches.

Place the needle in at the left dot next below and under the straight stitch. Bring the point out at the same level at the center dot.

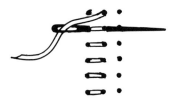

4. At the bottom horizontal stitch bring the needle out all the way to the right at the bottom right dot.

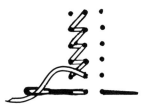

5. For the last side of the triangle and the last half of its base you will work back up the row. Bring the thread around by putting the needle in at the center bottom dot and out at the right bottom dot.

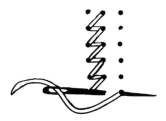

6. The needle goes into the fabric at the center dot next above, across horizontally, and out at the right dot.

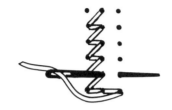

Repeat instructions 5 and 6 to the top of the row.

Four-Sided Stitch

DESCRIPTION

The Four-Sided Stitch is a series of squares in a horizontal line, end on end, with one edge in common. The row is worked from left to right.

To keep the line of squares straight keep the fabric taut on the hoop, pull the thread through fairly tightly, and take care where on the dot you place the needle. Each guidemark dot is sewn through more than once, which makes where you place the thread on each dot very important.

The wrong side of the fabric will look like the Cross-Stitch after you have completed this stitch.

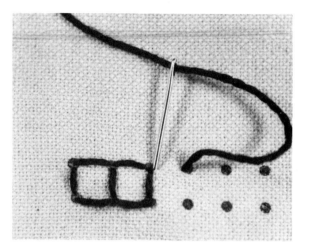

GUIDEMARKS

Two parallel horizontal rows of dots.
The rows are a quarter inch apart.
The dots are a quarter inch apart.

PROCEDURE

1. Bring the thread up just below the center of the leftmost, top-row dot. Place the needle into the fabric at the top of the dot directly below.

2. Bring the needle out at the next right top-row dot, on the left side of the dot.

3. The needle now goes into the fabric back one dot to the left. Place it to the right of the top of the straight stitch already there.

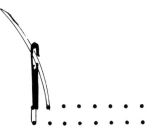

4. Bring the thread out on the left side of the next bottom-row dot to the right. Try to get it level with the bottom of the previous vertical stitch.

5. Place the needle into the fabric at the right side of the bottom-row dot next to the left.

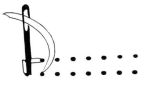

6. Bring the needle out at the bottom center of the top-row dot at the right end of the horizontal thread.

7. Complete the square by placing the needle in at the top center of the bottom-row dot below.

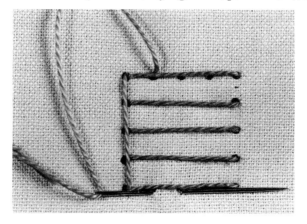

Continue the row, repeating the instructions from step two.

Open Laid Work

DESCRIPTION

Open Laid Work is a series of straight stitches running in both horizontal and vertical directions and spaced equal distances apart so that they form squares. The crossing threads at the corners of the squares are then tied down by another stitch. (See next Tying the Open Laid Work.)

GUIDEMARKS

A square of dots an inch on each side.
The dots are a quarter inch apart.
There are five dots on each side of the square.

PROCEDURE

1. Bring the thread up at the dot on the bottom right corner and across the whole bottom row of dots. Place the needle in at the left-most bottom dot and then out at the dot directly above.

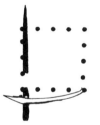

2. Bring the thread back all the way across the big square to the opposite dot on the right. Place the needle into the fabric going straight up. The needle will come out at the dot next above.

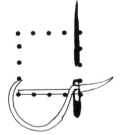

3. Continue forming these horizontal bars of thread, alternating from side to side until you get to the top row. Place the needle in at the top left dot and out at the bottom left corner of the big square. The needle should come out slightly to the left and below the horizontal thread at that bottom corner dot.

4. Place the needle in at the top left corner of the square to form a vertical bar and out one dot to the right to start the next stitch. Since the dots are now covered by thread your needle will come out just above the original dot.

5. Place the needle in opposite at the bottom edge of the square. Continue working back and forth from left to right to the top right corner.

Tying the Open Laid Work

PROCEDURE

1. Bring the thread out to the left an eighth inch above the bottom left corner of the square of Open Laid Work threads. Place the needle into the fabric diagonally across the corner just below and to the right of that left bottom edge of the square.

2. The next diagonal tie will be at the intersection of the next set of threads to the right. The needle comes out to the left and above the place where the threads intersect. Bring the thread across diagonally and into the fabric below at a distance from the intersection equal to that above.

Continue to the right end of this row. When you finish the row the thread will be behind the fabric at the right lower edge.

3. Bring the needle out straight above so that it is just below the horizontal thread of the next row of Open Laid Work. Turn the fabric

halfway around (180°) so the thread is now at the left of the square, and continue by repeating the directions from step one.

4. When you come to the end of the next row turn the fabric *before* you bring the needle up to begin the following row.

Other Stitches for Tying Open Laid Work

Cross Stitch (page 35)
French Knot (page 145)
Running Stitch (page 23)

Cross-Stitch

DESCRIPTION

The Cross-Stitch is a symmetrical cross of thread that looks like the letter

X. The threads of every stitch should cross in the same direction. It is most easily done in long rows of a color. The rows are worked as a series of diagonals from bottom to top and then back down forming the opposite diagonal by placing the needle through the prevous stitches.

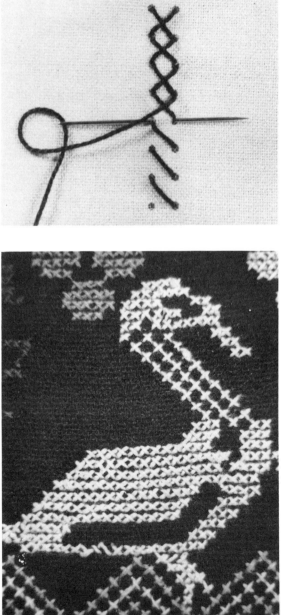

Detail of embroidered shawl from Mitla, Mexico.

GUIDEMARKS

Two parallel vertical lines of dots.
The dots are a quarter inch apart.
The lines are a quarter inch apart.

PROCEDURE

1. Pull the thread through the fabric at the bottom right dot.

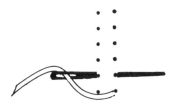

2. Place the needle into the fabric at the left dot next above, through the fabric horizontally, and out at the right dot opposite. What you are doing is taking a single Running Stitch between these two dots.

3.   Pull the needle through and continue the row by taking another horizontal Running Stitch at the dots next above. Repeat this to the top of the row of guidemark dots.

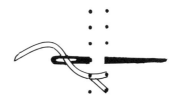

4.   Now you will start to work your way down the row to complete each Cross-Stitch. Embroider another Running Stitch starting at the left dot next below and bringing the needle out opposite at the bottom of the last diagonal thread.

5.   Continue down the row, covering diagonals by placing the point of the needle in at the left top of the previous stitch and out at the right bottom of the diagonal you are crossing.

6. After you have finished the row turn the fabric over and notice the wrong side. If you have been working correctly it will look like a series of double horizontal bars.

To work a single Cross Stitch, follow steps one and two and then merely place the needle back into the fabric at the bottom left dot to complete the cross.

Stem Stitch

DESCRIPTION

The Stemstitch is a rounded thickened line of thread. It is also called the *Outline Stitch* as it is often used to outline a shape or a group of another stitch. It can be used as a filling too and gives a rough, uneven textured look. It is quite easy to do since it is merely a Running Stitch with the stitches moved close together and slanted or rolled to give the look of in-

creased height. When Stem-stitching a round shape, place the guidemark dots closer *together*. Stitching on a curve requires stitches small enough so they do not separate and lose the solid outline look.

GUIDEMARKS

A horizontal line of dots.
The dots are a quarter inch apart.

• • • • • • • •

PROCEDURE

1. Begin with the thread at the rightmost dot. Place the needle into the fabric at the bottom edge of the second dot to the left.

Hold the loose thread out of the way below the guidemark with your right thumb to make it easier to see where to bring the needle out.

Bring the needle out just above the next dot to the right and pull it through.

2. Continue the line of stitches by placing the needle into the fabric slightly below the dot to the left of the stitching. Bring the needle out just above and to the right of the end of the previous stitch. Pull it through. The slight angle at which you place the needle is what creates the rounded three-dimensional look.

Split Stitch

DESCRIPTION

A straight stitch with a second thread coming up through its center half-way along its length. This straight stitch mimics a narrow chain. It is only one thread wide, which makes it the narrowest outline stitch you can embroider. The one thread is actually spit in half as the thread comes up through it in the second part of the stitch. A frequent use for the Split-stitch is to underline other stitches. As an underlining it is often embroidered around a circle or curve. (See notes below for a rounded Split stitch)

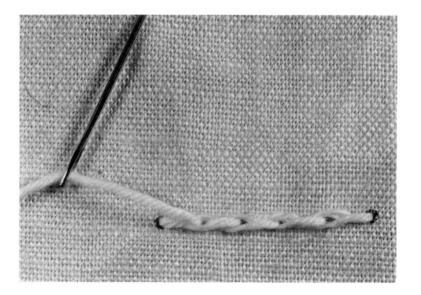

GUIDEMARKS

A straight horizontal line of dots an eighth inch apart.

•••••••••••••••••

PROCEDURE

1. With the thread at the right dot, place the needle into the fabric two dots to the left. You now have a straight stitch sitting flat on the fabric.

2. Bring the needle up one dot back to the right and through the dot and the middle of the thread that covers it. Keeping the thread and fabric taut will help you to spear and split the thread easily.

3. Before starting the next stitch, gently pull the threaded needle to the left. Pulling this splitting thread forward will split the flat thread even more and create the narrow chain-loop look.

4. Place the needle into the fabric at the next uncovered dot to the left. Again you have a flat straight stitch to spear. Notice that this time the needle will be brought up just at the end of the previous stitch.

Notes for a rounded Split stitch:

On a curved shape the flat stitch of step one will lie straight between two points on the curve. When you spear the stitch you will also be pulling it back to conform with the shape of the curve. Keep the flat stitch loose enough so that there is slack to pull back. Then use your right thumb to roll the thread up to the curve as your left index finger guides the point of the needle out from under the fabric.

Couching

DESCRIPTION

Couching is the tacking down of one thread by stitching it to the fabric with a second. Often Couching holds down a heavy cord with a comparatively thin embroidery thread. Couching gives you the opportunity to use materials that would be impossible to pull through fabric for any embroidery stitching, such as tinsel, string, silk braid, and loopy mohair knitting yarn. The color of the couching thread can also play a part in the look of the finished stitch. A thin thread the same color as a piece of fluffy mohair yarn will disappear, embroidery thread of a contrasting color and near the same thickness as the couched thread will stand out as part of the design.

The two simplest Couching stitches, described below, are Straight and Slanted Couching. The first anchors the cord with a straight vertical stitch, the second with a diagonally slanted thread. There are other stitches described in this book that can be used for Couching. You can embroider these stitches over a held-down cord or embroider the stitch first and then thread the cord through under the finished row of stitches.

You may want to hide the ends of the cord to be couched beneath the fabric. If it is possible, thread the cord through a large-eyed needle and bring it through the fabric; if not, make a hole with a sharp pencil point or scissors. Use the same point to push the cord through before you start couching it. When you have finished couching it, bring the other end of the cord through the fabric in the same way. On the other hand, you might choose to leave the raw ends of the couched cord sitting on top of the fabric; if so, place some clear drying glue on the ends to prevent them from raveling.

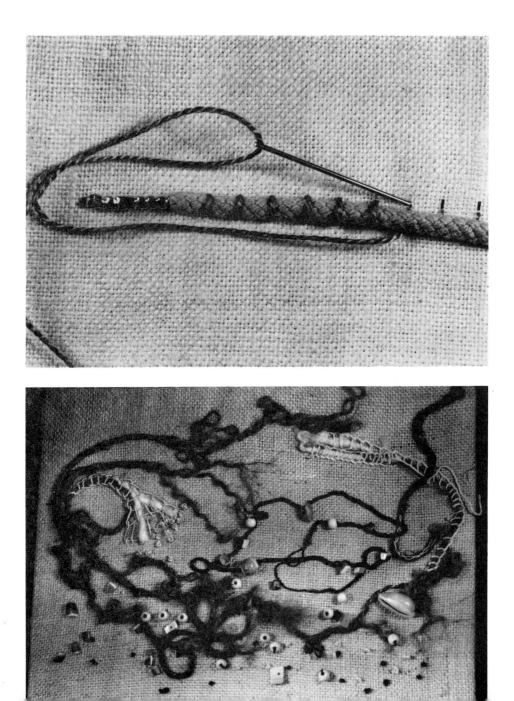

Other stitches used for Couching

Ladder Stitch (page 95)
Zig-Zag Chain Stitch (page 102)
Herringbone Stitch (page 121)
Basket Stitch (page 127)
Buttonhole Stitch (page 79)
One-Sided Feather Stitch (page 75)

GUIDEMARKS

A horizontal line with dots along it every quarter inch.

Hold the cord to be couched along the guidemarks.

Check to see if the dots are visible above and below; elongate the dots so they can be seen clearly from both sides.

Most often you will not be couching along a straight line. Generally you will decide where you want the thread to be couched to lie, then draw the guidemarks along that line.

PROCEDURE

1.   Hold the cord you are anchoring down in place along the guide-marks with your right thumb. Bring the embroidery thread up at the leftmost dot, below the cord.

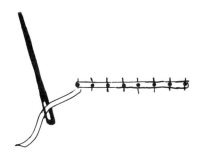

2.   For a *Straight Couching Stitch* bring the needle over the cord and place it into the fabric at the other side of the same dot. Slant the needle downward and to the right to come out below the cord at the next dot to the right. Pull the needle through so the couching thread is holding the cord down tightly.

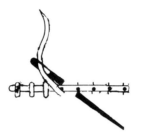

3.   For a *Slanted Couching Stitch,* instead of placing the needle into the fabric above and opposite where it comes out, place it in at the dot above the cord next to the right.

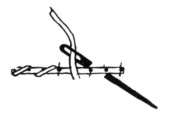

Sheaf Filling

DESCRIPTION

Three straight stitches pulled together at the center by a short straight "tacking stitch." The Sheaf Filling looks like a bundle of grain; it is used in embroidered pieces to represent sheaves. The stitch can also be used in rows as a decorative geometric. The instructions are for a row of sheaves. Embroidering the sheaves lying on their sides allows the needle to go into the fabric from left to right, the lefthanded direction, for most of the stitch. The two other straight-stitch threads of each sheaf must be lax enough for available slack to pull the threads toward the center with the tacking stitch.

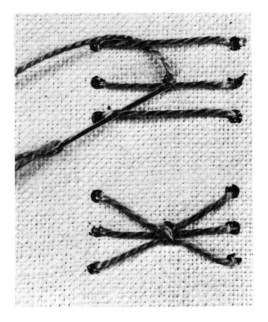

GUIDEMARKS

Mark two parallel vertical rows of three dot groups.

The rows are a half inch apart.

The groups are separated by a quarter inch.

The dots within the groups are an eighth inch apart.

Place a center dot halfway between the 2 rows in the center of each three-dot group.

PROCEDURE

1. With the thread coming out of the fabric from the bottom right dot, start the first of the straight stitches by placing the needle in at the bottom left dot.

2. The needle goes diagonally across behind the fabric to come out at the right dot next above the thread. Pull the thread through, and sew a second straight stitch like the first above it.

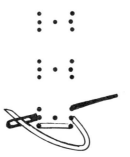

3. Complete the third straight stitch by putting the needle in at the top left dot and bringing it out at the center dot.

4. Pull the needle through, then slide it under the top thread. Bring the needle over the three straight stitches and under the bottom thread. Place the needle into the fabric at the center dot, and pull it tightly through for the entire stitch to come together.

5. To start the next stitch, continuing the row, bring the needle out again at the bottom right dot of the next three-dot group.

Satin Stitch

DESCRIPTION

The Satin Stitch is a group of raised straight stitches sewn so closely together that the threads come to resemble a shiny fabric surface. This look is achieved when threads are exactly parallel and pulled through with an equal tension so that they are all the same height. The Satin Stitch gets its height by being underlined with a second stitch, commonly the Running Stitch or the Split Stitch are used. The Split Stitch gives greater height than the Running Stitch. The Satin Stitch is the classic crewel embroidery stitch used to fill a variety of shapes.

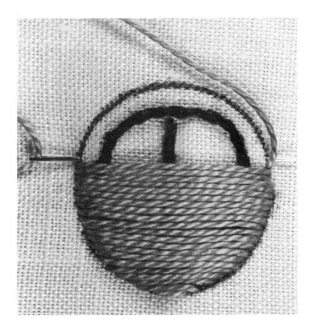

GUIDEMARKS

A circular shape. Trace a coin.

Just inside the perimeter mark a series of regularly spaced dashes.

Mark dashes down the center of the shape.

Place a straight edge across the center of the circle and mark a dot at each edge, these are the "starting dots."

PROCEDURE

1. Embroider the underlining stitch along the dashed guide. It is not necessary to use the same thread for the underlining stitch and the satiny portion. In fact, underlining with a contrasting color thread will show only if your satin threads are not close enough together. The thickness of the underlining thread will also be a factor in determining the height of the finished Satin Stitch.

2. Bring the embroidery thread out of the fabric at the Starting Dot on the right and in at the one on the left. This horizontal stitch is important because it sets precisely both the direction and the tension that every other thread in the shape will follow.

3. Bring the needle up close to the previous thread on the right side of the guidelines. Keep the second stitch close enough to the first so that no fabric or underlining thread shows through.

4.   Place the needle into the fabric on the left side of the shape above the last stitch at the same height on the shape as the right thread. Continue working up the outline of the shape with the stitches getting smaller until you reach the top. Be careful about keeping the threads parallel.

5.   Turn the fabric halfway around (180°). Start working again at the center of the shape, embroidering straight stitches following the outline upward. Embroidering from the longest stitches first helps insure that at least the major part of the shape has threads that are horizontal. If your stitches start to tilt as you go along it won't happen until you get to the short stitches, where it will be less visible.

Embroidery Picture, worked by M. Hull. American, dated Feb. 16, 1733. *Courtesy, Museum of Fine Arts, Boston*

Leaf Detail from wide Bed Curtain, Ipswich, Massachusetts. Most of the filling stitches on the leaf are Detached Chain (see page 91). *Courtesy, Museum of Fine Arts, Boston*

2  FEATHERS

Straight Feather Stitch

DESCRIPTION

Each stitch is a widened lopsided loop. The outer edge of the loop is straight but the second leg is angled toward the center and anchored in the top of the previous loop. This connects the loops in the row.

A vertical row of Straight Feather Stitches has straight outer sides of up and down alternating thread dashes connected by a series of back and forth threads, forming "v" 's.

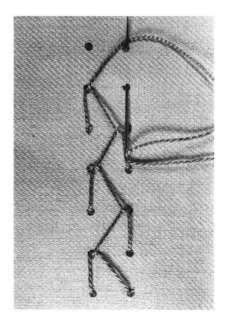

GUIDEMARKS

Two parallel rows of dots.
The rows are a quarter inch apart.
The dots are a quarter inch apart.

. .
. .
. .
. .
. .
. .

PROCEDURE

1. Start with the thread coming out of the fabric at the bottom right dot. Hold the thread flat across the fabric upward, going from right to left, so that it is between the left dots that are one and two levels above the thread, using your right thumb and index finger from the front and back to hold the thread.

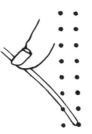

2. Place the needle into the fabric at the left dot directly opposite the emerging thread and out one dot above. As you pull the needle through notice that holding the thread with your right hand keeps you from pulling too tightly.

3.   Using the next two vertical dots on the right this stitch will be repeated. Bring the thread across, this time from left to right, and hold it above the second vacant dot above with your right thumb and forefinger (it is easier to see them from the front and back of the fabric at this edge of the stitch). Create the outer straight stitch as you did before, placing the needle in at the right dot and out one dot above. Continue to work back and forth, ending with a short tacking stitch to tie the last loop.

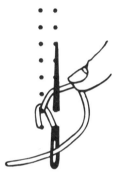

Closed Feather Stitch

DESCRIPTION

The edges of the stitch form two straight line rows. Between the edges are equal length straight stitches going back and forth in "V" formation. The individual stitches could be described as equal-sided triangles with their base forming the edge and the top point of each triangle facing in an alter-

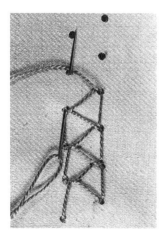

nating direction. This is a Straight Feather Stitch with the loops moved close enough together to touch. To help form regular triangles make sure the thread is held tightly under the needle before you pull it through.

GUIDEMARKS

Two vertical parallel rows of dots.
The rows are a quarter inch apart.
The dots are a quarter inch apart.
The right row is an eighth inch higher than the left.

PROCEDURE

1. Start with the thread from the bottom right dot. Place the needle into the fabric at the bottom left dot and the point out straight above. Place the thread under the point, keeping it straight and taut, and pull the needle through.

2. Place the needle into the fabric at the right bottom dot, just above the original thread. Bring the point of the needle out at the next dot above. Carry the thread under the needle point, and hold it down to

the right of the needle with your right thumb. Pull the needle through, passing over the held-down thread.

3. Repeat the stitch on the left side, putting the needle in at the last threaded dot and out one dot straight above. End the row by holding down the last loop with a small tacking stitch.

Squared Feather Stitch

DESCRIPTION

Each stitch is two right triangles with their long sides together. The row of Squared Feather Stitches looks like a vertical series of squares each cut in half by a diagonal thread, the squares are sitting one atop another. This is embroidered exactly like the Closed Feather Stitch, the difference being that the guidemark dots in the two rows are at the same horizontal level.

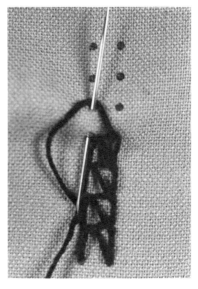

GUIDEMARKS

Two vertical parallel rows of dots.
The dots in the two rows are directly opposite each other.
The rows are a quarter inch apart.
The dots are a quarter inch apart.

PROCEDURE

1. The thread comes out of the fabric at the bottom right dot. Place the needle in at the bottom left dot and out straight above, one dot

higher. Bring the thread around under the needle point from right to left, pull the needle through.

2.   Hold the thread out horizontally to the right under your right thumb. Place the needle into the fabric at the bottom right dot. Bring the needle out one dot directly above and over the horizontal thread you are holding. This will create the common horizontal side for the series of squares.

3.   Continue the row, placing the needle in at the left dot where the

last threads show. End the row with a short tacking stitch over the last loop.

Slanted Feather Stitch

DESCRIPTION

An open loop with equally slanted sides. It is a double row of open loops at alternating levels. With rounded tops and open bottoms, they zig-zag from the sides of an imagined center line. The loops are linked by having the inside leg of each at the top center inside the last lower level loop. A row of these attractive stitches is done by turning the fabric at an angle and alternating horizontal and then vertical straight stitches. A use of the Slanted Feather Stitch is to act as a bridge, holding two pieces of fabric together, as in the traditional Crazy Quilt patchwork.

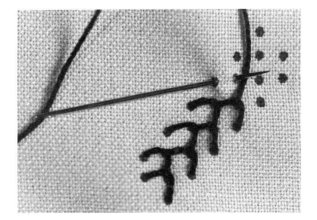

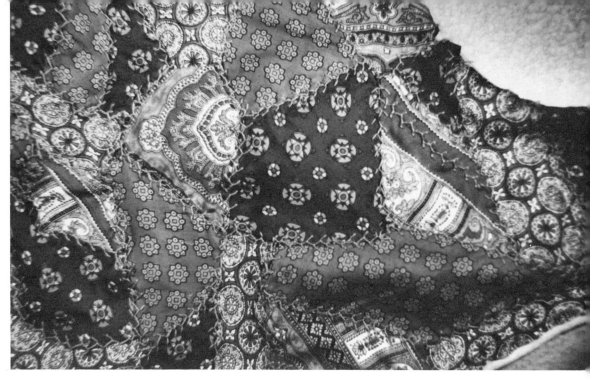

Man's Vest made of silk ties. Crazy quilt patchwork with the patches held together by Slanted Feather Stitch.

GUIDEMARKS

> Four vertical rows an eighth inch apart each with the same number of dots.
>
> The dots are a quarter inch apart.
>
> The rows alternate at the level at which they start.
>
> The second and fourth rows are an eighth inch below the other two.
>
> After you have created the guidemarks turn the fabric so that you will be embroidering on a diagonal going from bottom left to upper right.

PROCEDURE

1. Bring the thread up at the leftmost bottom dot. Place the needle into the fabric at the dot below and next to the right with the point coming up at the dot one level above to the right of the thread. Bring the thread under the needle point going from left to right, and pull the needle through.

2. Next is a horizontal stitch between the two leftmost dots next above. Bring the thread under the needle point from right to left and pull the needle through.

3. Now a vertical stitch the same as in step one. This is again done starting at the dot at the level below and coming out at the dot to the right of the previous loop. Bring the thread under the needle point going from right to left, and pull the needle through. Continue by repeating steps two and three and ending with a small tacking stitch over the last loop. Holding the thread under your right thumb after you have brought it under the needle point may insure an equal degree of tightness in the stitches.

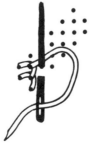

Spined Feather Stitch

DESCRIPTION

A series of open bottomed loops with one side of the loop forming a straight edge and the other spread so that it is out at an angle to the side. The straight edges are at the center of the row of stitches with the angled thread coming out from alternating directions. Each stitch starts from the top of the one below it. Working from side to side like this means that the straight side of the stitch is slightly to the left or right of the loop below it and this gives the spiny effect. The closer together the guidemark dots are placed the more pronounced the spine becomes.

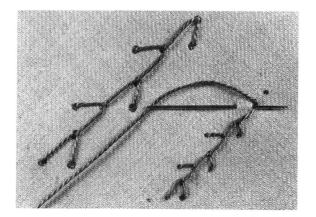

GUIDEMARKS

Three rows of dots.
The rows are an eighth inch apart.
The dots on the two outer rows are a half inch apart.
The dots in the center row are a quarter inch apart.
The rightmost row of dots starts an eighth inch above the center row,
    and the leftmost row an eighth inch below.

After marking the dots turn the fabric so that you can embroider, at an angle. The guidemarks will now look like a series of steps.

PROCEDURE

1.   Bring the thread up at the bottom left dot. The first stitch will be a vertical stitch between the bottom right dot and that directly above it. Once you have the needle in this position, place the thread under its point from left to right and hold it down under your right thumb for the proper thread tension while you pull the needle through.

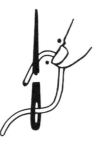

2.   The second stitch is a horizontal placing of the needle between the leftmost two dots next above. Again, holding the thread out to the right under your right thumb will make placing the needle easier. If you hold the thread parallel to the line of dots, above the set where the needle will go through, it will be in place for pulling the needle through.

3.   Continue with a vertical stitch starting at the dot to the right. If you hold the thread under your right thumb, to the right and above the dot where the needle will emerge, you can just pull the needle straight through, without having to carry the thread under the needle point. Continue by repeating steps two and three and ending with a horizontal tacking stitch.

Winged Feather Stitch

DESCRIPTION

A group of three long-legged one-sided Slanted Feather Stitches. Within the group the leg of each stitch gets progressively longer as it goes away from the center. The group then repeats itself on the other side of the center, in the opposite direction. The total effect is of birds' wings.

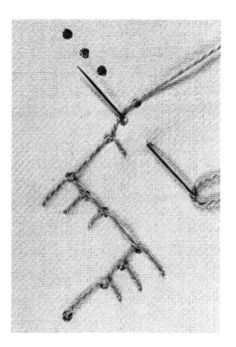

GUIDEMARKS

A series of three-dot groups perpendicular to each other.

The dots within each group are an eighth inch apart.

There is a quarter inch and a right angle between the top of one group and the bottom of the next.

Place a "starting dot" a quarter inch below the bottom group.

PROCEDURE

1. Turn the fabric so that the guidemarks are horizontal. Start with the thread coming up from the "starting dot." With your right thumb hold the thread against the fabric above the first three-dot group.

2. Place the needle into the fabric an eighth inch below the first dot of the group. Bring the point up at the dot and over the thread. Pull the needle through.

3.   Place the needle into the fabric below the second dot at a spot below the first stitch with the point coming out at the dot. Pull the needle through, making sure it passes over the held-down thread. Repeat this at the third dot, increasing the length of the stitch again.

4.   Turn the fabric so that the guidemarks are vertical. Hold the thread under your thumb above the next row of dots and continue by following instructions from step two.

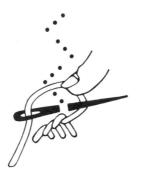

Chicken Tracks

DESCRIPTION

A series of wide-open loops zig-zagging from side to side with a central thread tracing the path of the zig-zag. Just think of a fat old fowl with matchstick legs waddling from side to side as she walks, these are the tracks she makes. Each footprint is made by embroidering two feather stitches—one slanted, one straight—with the top of the loops at the same point. These footprint stitches weave from side to side of the central thread line.

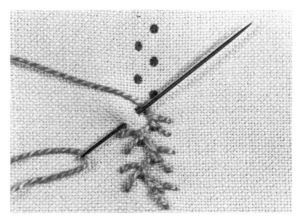

GUIDEMARKS

Two horizontal rows of dots.
The rows are an eighth inch apart.
The dots are separated by a quarter inch.
The lower row of dots is an eighth inch to the left of the upper.

PROCEDURE

1. Holding the fabric so that the guidemarks are horizontal, bring the thread up at the leftmost dot. Place the needle into the fabric about an eighth inch out from the dot, at an angle. With the thread under the needle point, pull the needle through at the dot.

2. Place the needle into the fabric an eighth inch directly below the same dot. Bring the needle out at the dot. With the free thread held under the needle point pull the needle through.

3. Turn the fabric so the guidemarks are vertical. Hold the thread above the next dot. Place the needle into the fabric at an angle, an eighth inch out from the dot. Pull the needle through and over the thread you are holding.

4. Continue by holding the thread above the same dot. Place the needle into the fabric an eighth inch to the left of the dot. Bring the point out at the dot so that you have a straight horizontal stitch. Pull the needle through. Turn the fabric so the guidemarks are again horizontal and continue from step one.

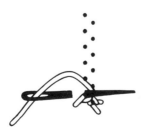

Pompidor

DESCRIPTION

The Pompidor is five one-sided Feather Stitches worked around a curve. The stitches increase in length to the third stitch, then decrease. Each group of five stitches curves in the direction opposite to the one before it. This stitch has a serpentine look as it curves back and forth. These directions use half-circles for guidemarks. You may want to try using curves that are not quite so rounded.

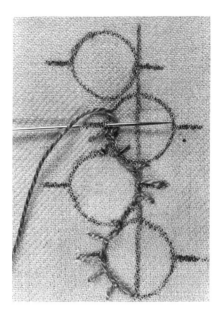

GUIDEMARKS

A series of circles sitting one atop the other.

Trace a dime, then with a ruler draw a vertical line through the center, straight up.

Place the dime above the circle just created and so that the right edge
of the coin touches the straight center line.

Trace the dime again with the straight center line going through its
center.

Lay the ruler across the horizontal of each circle and draw a straight
line a quarter inch out from each side of the circle.

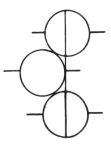

PROCEDURE

1.   Bring the thread up a short distance to the left of the bottom
center line. Place the needle into the fabric perpendicular to the curve
an eighth inch out and a third of the way between the thread and the
horizontal line. Bring the point out at the curve. Make sure the needle
passes over the thread; pull the needle through.

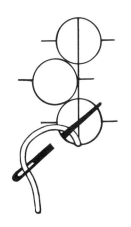

2.   Place the needle into the fabric halfway between the last stitch
and the horizontal thread. Make this stitch longer than the last. Hold
the free thread flat along the curved line. Pull the needle through
at the curved line, passing over the held-down thread.

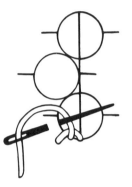

3.   Hold the thread with your right thumb just above the horizontal
halfway mark. Place the needle into the fabric at the halfway mark.
Pull the needle through at the curved line. Turn the fabric so the
guidemarks are horizontal, and embroider two more shorter stitches
between here and the top of the circle exactly like those in steps one
and two.

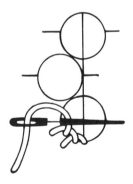

4.   Turn the fabric a quarter of the way around (90°) so the guide-marks are still horizontal but facing the other direction. Embroider the first three stitches as you did before. Turn the fabric again so that it is upside-down from its original position. Embroider the last two stitches. Turn the fabric so that it is back in its first position and continue from step one.

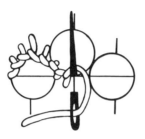

One-Sided Feather Stitch

DESCRIPTION

A series of open bottomed loops straight at one edge and sewn out at an angle at the other. The loops are connected at their straight edge forming a vertical thread line that has parallel diagonal threads coming off from it to the left.

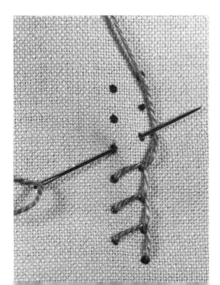

GUIDEMARKS

Two parallel vertical rows of dots.
The rows are a quarter inch apart.
The row on the right is an eighth inch lower than the left.

PROCEDURE

1.   Bring the thread up at the bottom right dot. Hold it out to the right under your right thumb.

2.   The needle goes in at the left bottom dot and diagonally across to come out at the next open right dot. Take the thread under your right thumb and roll it under the needle point. Hold the thread fairly taut as you pull the needle through.

Continue by repeating these steps; end with a short tacking stitch over the last loop.

"Tropical Leaves" by Hilda Kraus, Westport, Connecticut, wool on linen. *Courtesy, Mr. and Mrs. M. Fisher, Westport, Connecticut. Photo: Yvette Klein*

Bed Rug from the Wells-Thorn Museum House, Deerfield, Massachusetts. Blue and white. The surface of this hand-woven blanket is completely covered with a coarse darning stitch using from 2 to 5 strands of wool in 3 shades of indigo for the pattern. Background is darned in 8 strands of unbleached wool. Great variety is achieved by the number of background threads picked up or covered with the indigo. The knotted fringe is of deep indigo wool. *Courtesy, Historic Deerfield, Inc.*

3 ⚐ BUTTONHOLES

Classic Buttonhole Stitch

DESCRIPTION

A series of straight stitches held together at the top by a vertical line of thread. This line is called the "purl," the distinguishing mark of every type of Buttonhole Stitch. The stitch can be used to tuck under a hem, with the straight stitches the width of the hem. If you use it this way iron the hem in before you start embroidering.

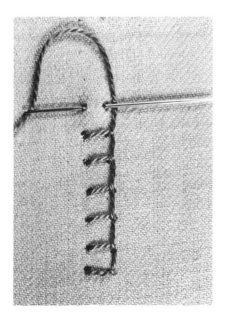

79

GUIDEMARKS

Two vertical rows of dots.
The rows are a quarter inch apart.
The dots are an eighth inch apart.

PROCEDURE

1.   Bring the thread up at the bottom right dot. Hold the thread out to the right under your right thumb. Place the needle into the fabric at the bottom left dot and out at the same right dot where the thread is. Pull the needle through passing over the held-down thread.

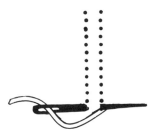

2.   Hold the thread out to the right above the next right dot. Place the needle in at the next available left dot and out straight across at the opposite right dot. Pull the needle through, being sure it passes over the thread you are holding down.

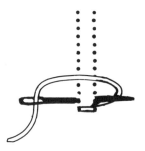

Round Buttonhole Stitch

DESCRIPTION

A circle of Buttonhole Stitches. It is shown here with the "purl" at the outer edge and legs of equal length. The length of the straight leg of the stitch may vary, and this will change the look of the stitch. A round buttonhole stitch with the "purl" at a small cut center is used in Drawn Fabric work or Broderie Anglaise.

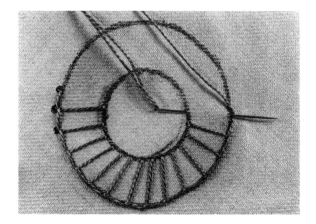

GUIDEMARKS

Trace a 25¢ coin.

Sketch an inner circle a quarter inch from the circle.

At the right side of the circle at "three o'clock" mark the starting dot, then mark two dots above this an eighth inch apart along the circle.

PROCEDURE

1.   Bring the thread up at the bottom starting dot. Hold the loose thread under your right thumb along the outside of the circle. Place the needle in at the inner circle opposite the starting dot. The needle point comes out at the second dot. The needle is pulled through, passing over the held-down thread.

2.   Turn the fabric slightly clockwise so that the stitch you have just created now sits where the starting dot was in step one. Repeat the step-one stitch. After the guidemark dots have been used, you will use your eye to approximate the same distances between the stitches and determine where you place the needle.

Closed Buttonhole Stitch

DESCRIPTION

A row of triangles with the bases connected and forming a vertical line. A variation on the Buttonhole Stitch, it has the two parallel legs moved together at their bottoms to form a triangle with the top bar. This is a useful stitch for tucking under a raw edge.

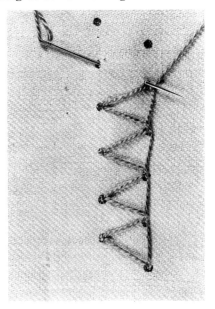

GUIDEMARKS

Two vertical rows of dots.
The dots are a quarter inch apart.
The right row is an eighth inch below the left.

PROCEDURE

1. Bring the thread out at the bottom right dot. Hold the thread out to the right under your right thumb. Place the needle into the

fabric at the bottom left dot and across going downward to come out at the first dot above the thread there. Pull the needle through.

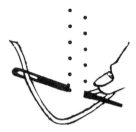

2. Place the needle into the fabric at the same bottom left dot. Bring it out at the next open right dot, pull it through, passing over the thread. Continue by repeating these two steps.

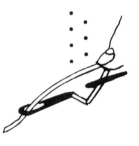

Lightning Buttonhole Stitch

DESCRIPTION

A triangular stitch of three equal sides with the base at the right edge of your embroidery. The working of this stitch is modeled on the closed Buttonhole Stitch but this is the short-cut version. It is done with a double strand of thread, but the stitches all come out as single threads.

These directions are for embroidering a row of stitches, each triangle faces the same direction with their bases, one atop the other, forming the "purl" at the right side of the stitch.

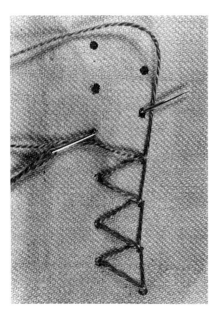

GUIDEMARKS

Two rows of dots.
The rows are a quarter inch apart.
The dots are a qarter inch apart.
The right row is an eighth inch below the left.

PROCEDURE

1.   Bring the double thread out at the bottom right dot. With your right thumb hold down one strand of the thread to the right of the guidemarks.

2.   Place the needle into the fabric at the bottom left dot. Bring it out at the next unoccupied right dot. Pull the needle through over the held-down thread. This means you are actually pulling the needle through between the two separated threads.

Buttonhole Chain Stitch

DESCRIPTION

A net of interlocking Buttonhole Stitches. The net is woven in rows using a Chain Stitch anchor on the outer edge of the shape you are embroidering. The Chain Stitch is embroidered to the fabric, the net of Buttonhole

Stitches merely covers the fabric. The entire net is very flexible and could be used for couching.

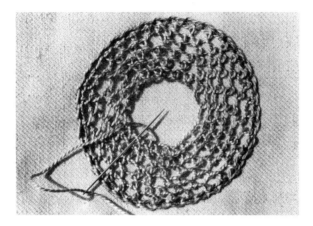

GUIDEMARKS

A circle the size of a twenty-five cent piece.

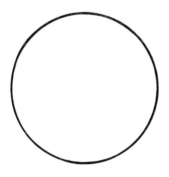

PROCEDURE

1. Embroider the Chain Stitch (page 93) along the guideline. When you have completed the chain, end the thread.

Bring the thread up in the center of a chain loop at the left side of the circle. This is the last time the needle should pierce the fabric until the ending stitch.

2. Place the needle under the inner side of the second chain loop clockwise from where the thread is now. Bring the thread under the needle point; hold it with your right thumb; pull the needle through. Notice that how tightly you pull the thread will determine the size of the stitch; try to get them all the same size.

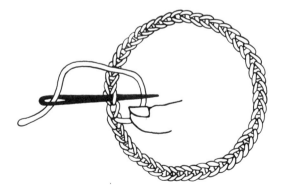

3. Continue embroidering unanchored Buttonhole Stitches through every other chain loop. When you have completed the Chain Stitch circle, continue by placing the needle through the loops of the Buttonhole Stitches you just created. As the circle of Buttonhole loops gets smaller and smaller skip one or two loops to make your row fit the circle size. After the entire space is covered, end by placing the needle into the fabric.

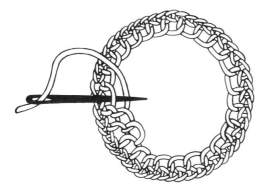

Crewel Embroidery Coverlet. Stitches: Buttonhole, Chain, Detached Chain, Herringbone, Satin, Roumanian, Running Stitch. *Courtesy, Wadsworth Atheneum, Hartford*

4  CHAINS

Detached Chain Stitch

DESCRIPTION

The Detached Chain Stitch is a vertical loop with a straight stitch coming up over the center top. The straight stitch is called a "tacking stitch" and serves the function of tying down the loop. A change in the length of the straight stitch will change the look of the stitch. The Detached Chain Stitch can be used singly or in groups to form branches and leaves or other shapes.

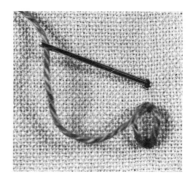

GUIDEMARKS

Three vertical dots.
The bottom two dots are a quarter inch apart.
The third dot is an eighth inch above the other two.

PROCEDURE

1. Bring the thread out on the right side of the bottom dot. Place the needle into the same dot on the left. Bring the point out at the bottom center of the next dot above; do not pull the needle through.

2. Use your right thumb to hold the thread out a short distance to the right. Push the needlepoint from the back with your right center fingertip so that it rises slightly from the fabric. Bring the loose thread around and under the needle from right to left; pull the needle through. Notice that the fullness of the loop decreases as you pull the thread more and more tightly.

3. Put the needle into the fabric at the last guidemark dot above the loop.

Chain Stitch

DESCRIPTION

The Chain Stitch is a series of thread loops linked one into another. The bottom of each loop starts within the full, round top of the one below. It is based on using a series of Detached Chain Stitches without the tacking stitch. Because the width and direction of the chain line can easily be varied, the Chain Stitch is used to outline areas and to fill in areas with closely worked rows. The width of the chain is determined by the distance between the guidemarks and the size of the loop, the direction in which you place the guidemark dots.

GUIDEMARKS

A vertical line of dots a quarter inch apart.

•
•
•
•
•
•

PROCEDURE

1.   Start as you did in the Detached Chain Stitch, with the thread coming from the right half of the bottom dot. Hold the thread out to the right with your right thumb. Place the needle in at the same dot to the left of the thread. Bring the point out at the *lower right* of the dot above. Do not pull the needle through.

2.   With your right center fingertip, from beneath the fabric, push the needlepoint out a little. Bring the free end of the thread under the needlepoint and pull the needle through. You will develop control of the width of the loop by how tightly you pull the thread and the amount of slack under your thumb.

3.   After the first loop, you are always embroidering over the threads of the previous loop. Start the next stitch from the left of the dot inside the thread loop. Continue forming loops as described in steps one and two.

4.   End the chain row with a tacking stitch over the top of the last loop.

Ladder Stitch

DESCRIPTION

The Ladder Stitch is a Chain Stitch with a large loop widened at both the top and the bottom so that it becomes almost squared. To achieve this effect the chain loop is spread across two rows of dots instead of being worked around a single row of guidemark dots. When the thread is pulled tight enough to give straight sides, a vertical row of this stitch looks like the sides and rungs of a ladder. In contemporary stitchery designs, the width and height of the rungs and sides might be varied to form irregular patterns (see photo page 44). For a ladder that is not square or symmetrical, vary the distance between the rows or between the guidemark dots. Use a square Ladder Stitch in close rows to form an airy filling. The Ladder Stitch can also be used for Couching by running a second thread under the ladder rungs.

GUIDEMARKS

Two parallel vertical lines of dots.
There is a quarter inch between the lines.
There is a quarter inch between the dots.

. .
. .
. .
. .
. .
. .

PROCEDURE

1.   With the thread at the center of the bottom right dot place the needle in at the bottom left dot and the point out at the next dot above to the right. Hold a short length of thread out to the right of the dot under your thumb. The needle is not pulled through.

2.   Carry the loose end of the thread under the needlepoint going from right to left. Pull the needle through, keeping the thread loose enough so that you have a large floppy loop that slants to the right.

3.   To spread the loop and start the next stitch place the needle into the fabric inside the thread loop at the dot to the left of the thread.

4.   Bring the point out at the right dot next above. After you pick up the thread and bring it under the needle point, give it a tug to the left. This slight pull will tighten the previous loop, using the needle as a form to pull against. End the row with a short tacking stitch from each dot over the loop.

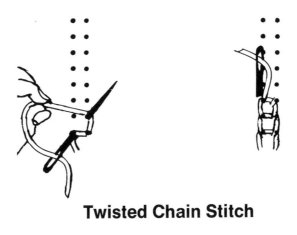

Twisted Chain Stitch

DESCRIPTION

This is a series of chained loops with the threads crossed at the base of the loop. The loop slants to the right, which makes the left thread longer than the right and accentuates the crossing loops. It has in common with the Ladder Stitch the separated base of the chain loop, but in the Twisted Chain Stitch only one leg is inside the previous loop.

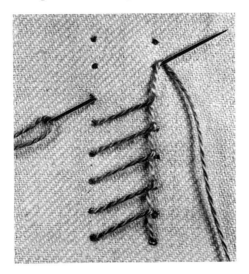

GUIDEMARKS

Two vertical lines of dots an eighth inch apart.
The dots are a quarter inch apart.

PROCEDURE

1.   Start a chain loop by bringing the thread out of the fabric at the bottom right dot. Place the needle into the fabric at the bottom left dot and the point out at the right dot diagonally above.

2.   Carry the thread so that it goes over the top of the needle and under the point from the left to the right. Pull the needle through.

3. Continue the Twisted Chain by placing the needle into the fabric at the left dot next to the top of the loop you have just completed.

Rope Chain Stitch

DESCRIPTION

A series of Twisted Chain loops worked very close to one another. The elongated left leg of the loop is brought out so far to the left that the loop itself acts like a small knot that raises one edge of the stitch. With one side raised, the row of parallel diagonal stitches is rounded and looks very much like a length of rope. As in the Satin Stitch, keeping the tension even and the long leg thread parallel is the secret of a goodlooking stitch. The guidemarks are simple because the first stitch becomes your guide for the others.

GUIDEMARKS

Two dots, placed horizontally a quarter inch apart.

• •

PROCEDURE

1. Bring the thread out of the fabric at the right dot. Place the needle in at the left dot and with the point out at the right edge slightly above the first thread. Bring the thread over the top of the needle and under the point from left to right. As you pull the needle through, recognize this as a squat Twisted Chain Stitch.

2. Place the needle into the fabric at the left above the last thread. The distance above the thread should be equal to the size of the loop you just created on the right. Bring the needle point out at the right just above the top of the previous loop, with the needle parallel to the last diagonal thread.

Zig-Zag Chain Stitch

DESCRIPTION

The Zig-Zag Chain Stitch is a series of chain loops placed at angles opposite one another—a Chain Stitch gone awry to form a back and forth line of loops. These slanted loops are tacked in place by the next stitch. Each loop has one of its bottom threads going through the top of the last loop.

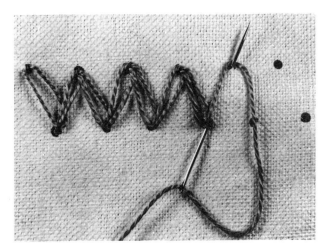
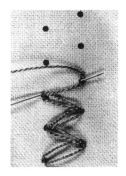

GUIDEMARKS

Two vertical rows of dots a quarter inch apart.
The dots are also a quarter inch apart.
The left row is an eighth inch below the right.

PROCEDURE

1. Start the first slanted loop by bringing the thread out at the bottom left dot. The needle goes in at the left of the same dot, and the point is brought out diagonally above at the bottom right uncovered dot. Bring the thread under the needle point from right to left as you did in the other chain stitches to form the loop. Pull the needle through.

2. Turn the fabric so that the guidemarks now face in a horizontal direction. Place the needle through the thread (and the dot under it) that forms the top of the last loop. The needle point comes out at the dot above and to the right. This time when you bring the thread under the point it will go from left to right (clockwise) to form the loop.

3. Turn the fabric back so the guidemarks are again in a vertical direction. Place the needle into the fabric through the top thread of

the last loop, anchoring it down as you continue, by taking the stitch
to the dot next above at the right.

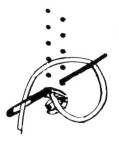

Zig-Zag Feather Chain Stitch

DESCRIPTION

A line of chain loops embroidered at right angles to each other. The loops
are connected by a back and forth straight stitch that zig-zags between the
loops. Both the distance between the loops and the connecting straight
stitch create a stitch that makes me think of a branch with leaves. Another
way of describing this stitch would be that it is a series of Detached Chain
Stitches with long tacking stitches. These Detached Chain Stitches are
placed at right angles one against another.

GUIDEMARKS

Four parallel lines of dots.

The lines are separated by an eighth inch.

The dots in each line are a quarter inch apart.

The second and fourth lines are an eighth inch lower than the other two.

The fabric is then turned so that the dots are angled from the bottom left upward to the right.

PROCEDURE

1. Start from the bottom right dot and embroider a chain loop to the left dot next above.

2. Place the needle into the fabric at the dot directly above for the tacking stitch.

3.   Bring the needle out at the dot to the left of the end of the tacking stitch. The needle goes in at the same dot, next to the thread. For a loop, the point comes out at the top of the last tacking stitch. Bring the thread under the needle point, and pull the needle through. This has given you a chain loop from the opposite direction.

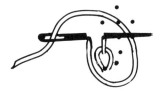

4.   Place the needle in at the dot directly to the right of the loop you just created. Continue by repeating the directions from step one.

Lazy Daisy Stitch

DESCRIPTION

The Lazy Daisy is a flower made by embroidering a series of detached chain stitches around a circle, each stitch is a petal.

GUIDEMARKS

A circle of eight dots with a dotted circle in the center. The diameter of the circle is a half inch.

1. Place the rule on the fabric vertically and mark three dots, one every quarter inch.

• • •

2. Turn the ruler so that it is now horizontal, but still going through the center dot. Again mark a dot a quarter inch each side of the center.

•
• • •
•

3. Rotate the ruler so that it is halfway between the two outer dots and going through the center. Mark dots a quarter inch either side of the center.

4. Turn the ruler opposite where it is and mark the last set of dots a quarter inch from the center. If you have been careful the eight dots of the circle will be equally spaced.

5. On the center circle mark a tiny dot opposite each outer dot.

PROCEDURE

1. With the thread at the inner circle dot in front of you, going to the dot above, embroider a Detached Chain Stitch that has a tacking stitch so short no top guide dot is needed.

2. Turn the fabric to the left so that the dots for the next stitch are now in front of you. If you do this before you place the needle in for the tacking stitch, as you tack down the loop the needle can come out on the inner circle dot for the next stitch. Otherwise bring the needle out at the next inner dot to the right and embroider another Detached Chain Stitch.

3. Continue these stitches all around the circle. When you finish the petals try filling the center of the flower with a Satin Stitch or a French Knot.

Wheat Ear

DESCRIPTION

A chain loop with two straight stitches holding it down from each side of the top. It could also be described as a series of Detached Chain Stitches with a double tacking stitch. The straight or tacking stitches are at an angle from the top of the loop and are long, relative to the size of the loop.

The stitches are placed one atop the other in a row.

The row of stitches looks like a stalk of wheat grains.

A single stitch brings to mind a rabbit's head with its long ears which is called the Bunny Stitch.

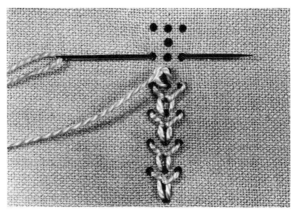

GUIDEMARKS

Three vertical parallel rows of dots.
The rows are an eighth inch apart.
The two outer rows have dots that are a quarter inch apart.
The center-row dots are an eighth inch apart.
The center row starts an eighth inch below the others and has two extra
dots at the bottom.

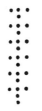

PROCEDURE

1.   Start the first chain loop from the bottom center dot. The needle point is brought straight up to the dot above it and out directly above where it went into the fabric (the left side of the dot). Bring the thread under the needle point for the loop, going from right to left. The loop will be slightly slanted to the left and should be full enough so that it can be spread slightly.

2.   Place the needle straight across between the two outer dots next above. Pulling the needle through will give you the first tacking stitch.

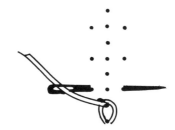

3.   For the second tacking stitch the needle goes into the fabric at the right side of the center dot within the loop.

4. Start the next stitch by bringing the thread up at the right half of the empty center dot between the tops of the two tacking stitches and repeat from step one.

Chain Cable Stitch

DESCRIPTION

This stitch is a series of rounded loops connected at the top and bottom by straight stitches sticking out from the loop. An old-fashioned link chain, it is similar to a series of Detached Chain Stitches embroidered in a vertical row. The technique used to embroider this stitch is to create simultaneously both the loop and the straight stitch by twisting the thread around the needle itself and placing the needle into the fabric only once per stitch.

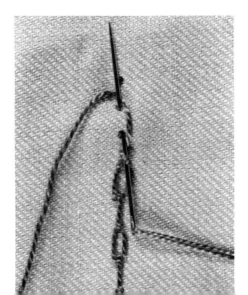

GUIDEMARKS

A vertical line of dots.
The dots are an eighth inch apart.

PROCEDURE

1.   Hold the thread with your right hand as it comes from the center of the bottom dot. Hold the needle in your left hand diagonally above the same dot, wrap the thread around the needle. It goes over the top of the needle in a clockwise direction.

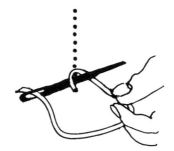

2.   Place the needle into the fabric at the next dot above. Pull the end of the thread you just wrapped around the needle so that it is close to the fabric, eliminating the slack.

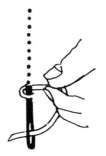

3. Bring the needle point out of the fabric at the next dot above.
Bring the thread under the needle point, going from right to left, and
pull the needle through. Continue the chain by repeating the instructions from step one.

Crewel Embroidery. Detail showing use of French Knots (see page 145). *Courtesy, Wadsworth Atheneum, Hartford*

5 "V" 'ed

Arrowhead Stitch

DESCRIPTION

Two diagonal threads come together in a point to form a V-shaped stitch. They sit one atop the other in the row. Each stitch is done in two steps. Keeping the stitches regular and of equal size makes a neat-looking row and is simply a matter of where you place the dots.

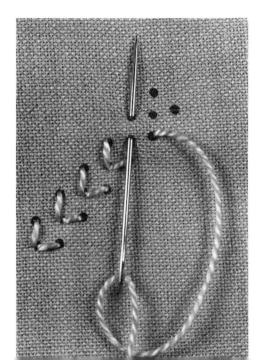

GUIDEMARKS

Three parallel rows of dots.
The rows are an eighth inch apart.
The center row is an eighth inch lower than the other two.
The dots within each row are a quarter inch apart.

PROCEDURE

1.   Turn the fabric so that the guidemarks are at a diagonal in front of you. Bring the thread out at the bottom right dot.

2.   Place the needle in at the dot to the left of the thread. Bring the needle out at the dot directly above.

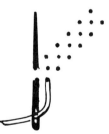

3. Place the needle into the fabric at the dot directly below, next to the thread which ends the half of the stitch you just created. Bring the needle through at the next free dot on the rightmost row.

Continue by repeating steps two and three.

Fern Stitch

DESCRIPTION

Two diagonal straight stitches meeting at one end to form a point, then one more stitch sticking up from the center of the point. The length and the width of the V may be varied as can the size of the straight stitch. These instructions are for a straight row of Fern Stitch. A group of curved rows will give the delicate feathery look of a fern. A short row with the width and length of the stitches increasing then decreasing and outlined with a Stemstitch looks like a hardwood leaf. The guidemarks are the same as those for the Arrowhead Stitch.

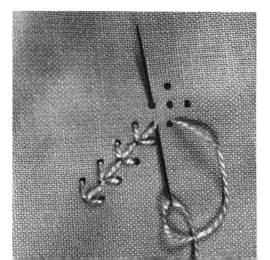

GUIDEMARKS

Three parallel vertical rows of dots.
The rows are an eighth inch apart.
The dots are a quarter inch apart.
The center row is an eighth inch below the other two.

PROCEDURE

1. Turn the fabric so that the guidemarks are at a diagonal in front of you. Bring the thread out at the bottom right dot.

2. Place the needle into the fabric at the dot to the left of the thread and out at the dot directly above.

3.   Put the needle into the fabric at the dot directly below next to the end of the thread. Bring the needle out at the center dot above.

4.   Place the needle into the fabric at the dot below the thread right in the point of the "V". Bring the needle through at the next available dot in the right row.

Fly Stitch

DESCRIPTION

A wide open "V" of threads with a straight stitch going up the center and then crossing the point of the "V". The row of Fly Stitches is embroidered on a horizontal going from left to right. It looks very much like the Fern Stitch with the center straight stitch moved back.

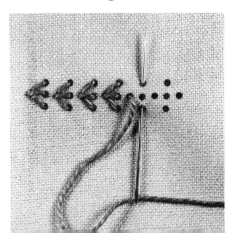

GUIDEMARKS

Three horizontal rows of dots.
The rows are separated from each other by an eighth inch.
The two outer rows have dots a quarter inch apart.
The center row has an extra dot at both the top and bottom.

PROCEDURE

1.   With the guidemarks horizontal in front of you, bring the thread out at the leftmost center dot.

2.   Take a vertical stitch from bottom to top between the two outer row dots next to the right.

3.   Place the needle into the fabric at the center dot where you started the stitch. Bring the needle through in a horizontal stitch one dot to the right.

Opposite: Detail and full view of an antique patchwork quilt from Cuttyhunk, Massachusetts.

4.   Place the needle into the fabric behind the point of the "V" at the dot where you started the stitch. Bring the needle out on the center row at the second dot to the right.

This completes a single Fly Stitch; continue the row by repeating directions from step two.

Herringbone Stitch

DESCRIPTION

A series of diagonal stitches between two horizontals which cross each other near the edges. This is like the Cross-Stitch except that the threads cross at alternate sides near the top or bottom of the diagonal stitch. The row is worked from right to left with the needle placed into the fabric in the left-handed direction from left to right.

The Herringbone Stitch and variations of it have been used by Americans for a long time. It is found in almost every example of antique Crazy-Quilt patchwork embroidery of the eighteenth and nineteenth centuries.

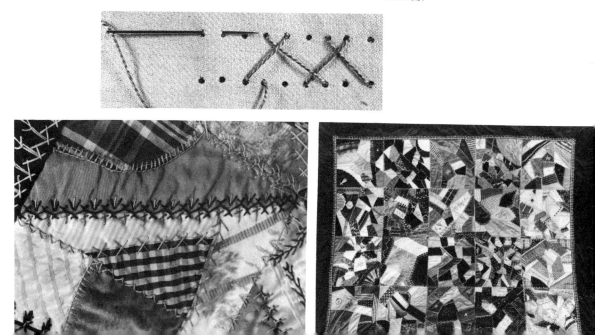

GUIDEMARKS

Two parallel horizontal rows of dots.
The rows are a quarter inch apart.
The dots within the row are an eighth inch apart.

. . . .
. . . .

PROCEDURE

1.   Bring the thread up from the rightmost lower dot. On the upper row make a straight stitch between the third and second dots from the right.

2.   Place the needle into the fabric on the bottom row of dots, three dots to the left of the last stitch embroidered on that row. Pull the needle through one dot to the right of where you placed it in.

3.   Place the needle into the fabric on the upper row three dots to the left of the last stitch embroidered on the row. Bring the needle through one dot to the right of where you put it in.

Continue working from upper to lower guidelines, repeating steps two and three to the completion of the row.

Spiked Herringbone Stitch

DESCRIPTION

A widened "X" of threads with the top right thread extended upward for a distance equal to half the height of the stitch. The stitch is easy to embroider, particularly if you can already do the Herringbone Stitch, for it is a Herringbone with one side extended upward spikelike.

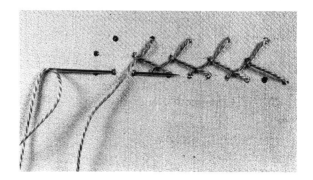

GUIDEMARKS

Three parallel horizontal rows of dots.
The rows are separated by an eighth inch.
The bottom row dots are an eighth inch apart.
The middle row dots are a quarter inch apart. The leftmost dot of
   this row is directly above the bottom row left dot.
The top row dots are a quarter inch apart. The dots start an eighth
   inch to the right of the other rows.

PROCEDURE

1. Bring the thread up at the bottom right dot. Place the needle into

the fabric at the center right dot and diagonally upward to come out at the top row right dot. Pull the needle through.

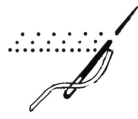

2. Holding the needle by the pointed end, slide it back under the stitch you have just created. Do not loosen the thread as you go under it.

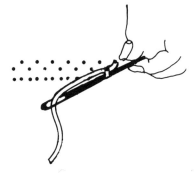

3. Place the needle into the fabric on the bottom row two dots to the left of the last stitch embroidered there. Pull the needle through one dot to the right of where you put it in. Continue from step one.

Chevron Stitch

DESCRIPTION

A Chevron Stitch row is a series of back and forth diagonal threads with a horizontal bar atop the upper and lower points. You might prefer to imagine the Chevron Stitch as a string of horizontal "V's" placed end on end with the tips and points of their "V's" having a bar on them.

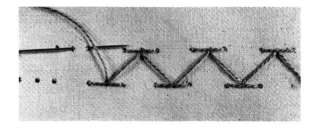

GUIDEMARKS

Two parallel horizontal rows of dots.
The rows are a quarter inch apart.
Each row is a series of three-dot groups.
The groups are a quarter inch apart.
The dots within each group are an eighth inch apart.
The bottom row is a quarter inch to the left of the top.
The bottom row has an extra "starting dot" directly below the right
    dot of the top row.

PROCEDURE

1. Bring the thread up at the "starting dot". Place the needle into the fabric at the center dot of the top right group of dots. Pull the needle through at the right dot of that same top group.

2.   Place the needle in at the left dot of the same top group. Bring the point out at the center dot, next to the stitch already there. As you pull the needle through, be sure that it comes out below the horizontal stitch being created.

3.   On the next bottom-row group of three dots, to the left, place the needle into the center dot and out at the right dot.

4.   Place the needle into the fabric at the left dot of the same group and out at the center dot. This time the horizontal thread must be below the stitch you are embroidering.

Variation

In steps two and four let the horizontal thread go onto the other side of the stitch, this will make the "V" cross the bar rather than be bounded by it.

Basket Stitch

DESCRIPTION

A series of diagonally placed straight stitches woven over and under each other between two parallel lines. Opposite threads overlap once near each edge and cross again at the center. The total effect is of basketry.

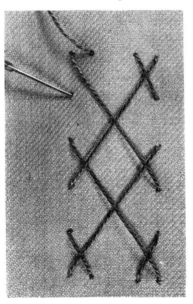

GUIDEMARKS

Two parallel vertical lines of dots.
The lines are a half inch apart.
The dots are a quarter inch apart.
There are starting and ending dots at the bottom and top of these lines. These dots are an eighth inch in at the top and bottom of the lines.

PROCEDURE

1.   Bring the thread out at the fourth dot up from the bottom of the right line of dots.

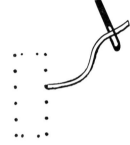

2.   The needle goes into the fabric at the bottom left guidemark dot and comes through straight across at the left starting dot.

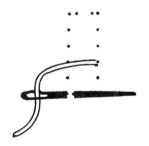

3.   Place the needle in on the left line at the second dot from the bottom and out straight across at the corresponding dot on the right line.

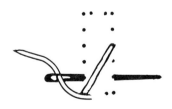

4.   Place the needle in at the right starting dot and out at the bottom right dot.

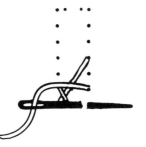

5.   Next, the needle goes into the fabric at the left-line dot directly opposite the top right thread. Bring the needle out at the right one dot below that top right thread.

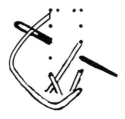

6.   At the second dot above the top thread take a horizontal stitch straight across.

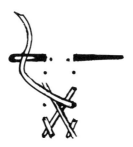

7. Place the needle into the fabric at the empty left dot three dots below. Bring the needle out on the right one dot below the top thread.

8. Repeat steps six and seven to the end of the row. To end the row, take a backward stitch, placing the needle in at the right-ending dot and out at the left-ending dot. Finish by placing the needle in at the last uncovered dot below on the left.

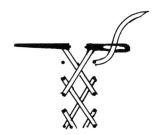

Vandyke Stitch

DESCRIPTION

A straight vertical row of Vandyke Stitches is a series of horizontal bars coming from a center-raised chain spine. The center spine is woven from crossing angled threads coming from opposite edges of the shape. As the needle goes under the threads, it pulls them to the horizontal, while creating the center chain. Of course the shape of the stitch can be changed by simply changing the shape of the guidelines.

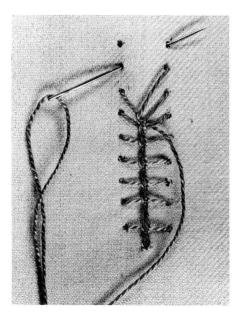

GUIDEMARKS

Two parallel vertical lines of dots.
The lines are a quarter inch apart.
The dots are an eighth inch apart.
A starting dot is placed an eighth inch below and between the bottom dots of the two rows.

PROCEDURE

1. Bring the thread up at the bottom dot on the right row of guide-marks. Place the needle in at the left of the starting dot and out on the right side of the same dot.

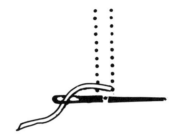

2. Place the needle into the fabric on the left bottom dot and bring it through the next free dot on the right.

3. Going straight across from left to right, place the needle under the crossed threads without going into the fabric.

Pull the thread tight.

Continue by repeating steps two and three.

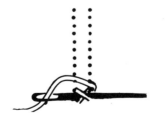

Cretan Catch Stitch

DESCRIPTION

A center zig-zag with spikes going off in alternating directions. The spikes are threads crossing each other as they are tacked down above and below an imaginary center line. To give tiny tacking stitches, you will be placing the needle in and out around the same dot.

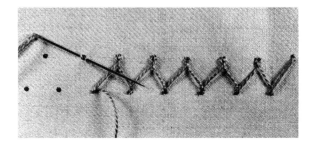

GUIDEMARKS

Two parallel horizontal lines of dots.
The dots in each line are a quarter inch apart.
The bottom line is an eighth inch to the left of the top.

PROCEDURE

1. Bring the thread up at the top right dot. Place the needle in at the bottom of the right bottom dot, bring it out just above the same dot.

Make sure the needle point passes over the free thread. then pull the
needle through.

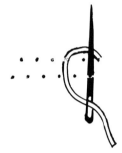

2.   Place the needle at the top left of the next upper row dot. Bring
the point out at the bottom right of the same dot. Pull the needle
through, making sure the free thread is below the needle.

6  SOLID

Cretan Stitch

DESCRIPTION

This is like a double horizontal Feather Stitch. It has a spidery edge with a woven center. The stitch starts as a Slanted Feather, but as you work your way up the circle the needle is inserted more and more horizontally; at the halfway point on the circle, it is exactly horizontal. After the halfway point, when embroidering the right half of the stitch, you will rotate the fabric 90 degrees in order to keep the needle going into the fabric in the left-handed directions.

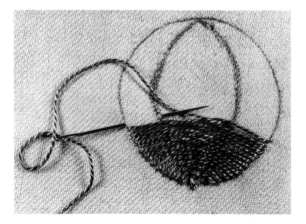

GUIDEMARKS

An ellipse within a circle.
Trace a 25¢ piece.
Sketch an ellipse within this shape.
Place a starting dot an eighth inch from the bottom center.

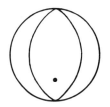

PROCEDURE

1.   Embroider a Detached Chain Stitch from the bottom center to the starting dot.

2.   Place the needle in at the left bottom of the circle about an eighth inch above the left of the last stitch. Bring the point out on the ellipse; with the thread under the needle point, pull the needle through.

3. Place the needle in at the right edge of the circle and out at the ellipse right. With the thread under the needle point, pull the needle through.

Fishbone Stitch

DESCRIPTION

A series of threads angled out from the center spine. The spine is a tacking stitch holding and anchoring the outward stitches.

GUIDEMARKS

An elliptical shape with a line up the center.
Two dots, a quarter inch apart, start at the bottom of the center line.

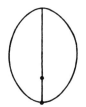

PROCEDURE

1.   Bring the thread up at the bottom dot. Place the point in at the next dot above, and bring it out near the bottom right of the ellipse.

2.   Place the needle in at the bottom left of the ellipse at about the same distance from the center as the thread is to the right.

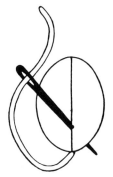

Bring the point out above the center straight stitch. Bring the loose thread under the needle point going from right to left. Pull the needle through.

3.   Place the needle in just above the thread loop you just created. Bring the point out at the right side of the ellipse a short distance above the previous stitch. Pull the needle through. Continue, repeating from step two.

Straight Fishbone Stitch

DESCRIPTION

A series of angled straight stitches coming from either edge of the shape and crossing each other at the center. A fish skeleton with the bones coming out at an angle from a central spine. The stitch may be done following the the outlines of any shape—an elongated ellipse will give a fish; a leaf shape can also be used. Embroider a veined leaf by changing the shape of the two outer rows of dots. If these rows become rounded instead of straight, the same stitch will have a whole new look.

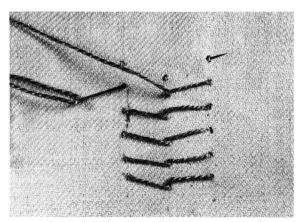

GUIDEMARKS

Three vertical rows of dots.
The rows are a quarter inch apart.
The dots are an eighth inch apart.
The center row is a sixteenth inch below the other two.

PROCEDURE

1. Bring the thread out at the bottom right dot. Place the needle into the fabric to the left of the bottom center dot, and bring it through at the right of the same dot.

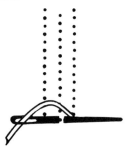

2. Place the needle into the fabric at the bottom dot of the left row. Bring the needle through to the next free bottom dot on the right row.

Place the starting dot an eighth inch from the bottom center of the shape.

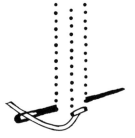

Closed Fishbone Stitch

DESCRIPTION

A tightly overlapping series of diagonally crossed threads. The threads cross in the center of the shape, coming to this point from opposite diagonals from either side. Each stitch is done close to the one before it.

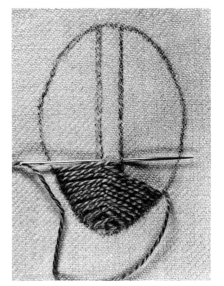

GUIDEMARKS

An elliptical shape with two parallel lines down the center.
Draw a leaf shape keeping both sides as symmetrical as possible.
Draw two vertical lines an eighth inch apart down the center of this
shape.

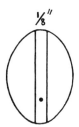

PROCEDURE

1. Start by bringing the thread up at the bottom center of the shape. Place the needle into the fabric at the starting dot and through on the outline at the bottom right of the parallel lines.

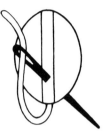

2. Take a straight horizontal stitch between the two vertical guide-mark lines halfway along the length of the first vertical straight stitch.

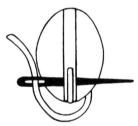

3. Place the needle in at the left bottom of the outline, as far up as you stitched on the right. Bring the needle through on the right edge of the outline just above the previous thread.

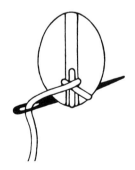

4. Take a horizontal straight stitch just above the crossed threads at the center lines. Continue by repeating steps three and four to fill the entire shape.

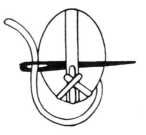

Roumanian Stitch

DESCRIPTION

A series of closely woven horizontal threads. The center of each thread has the appearance of being tied down by a second diagonal thread. You can change the shape of the stitch or the width of the center diagonal by varying the guidemarks. Placing the inner lines closer together will make a narrower diagonal. Curving all the lines outward will give a solid leaf shape. In early American embroidery this is known as New England Laid Work and was often used in place of Satin Stitch to save thread.

GUIDEMARKS

Four vertical parallel lines.
The two outer lines are a half inch from each other.
The two inner lines are an eighth inch from each of the outer lines.

PROCEDURE

1.   Bring the thread out at the bottom of the rightmost line.

Place the needle into the fabric at the bottom of the leftmost line and out straight across at the inner line next to the right.

Pull the needle through with the thread passing *above* the needle.

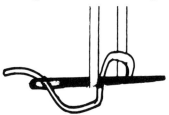

2.   Place the needle into the fabric at the inner left line just above the thread; bring it through at the far right line.

It is important for the stitches to be very close together, so that the stitch comes together to look well done.

Continue by repeating steps one and two, always almost touching the previous stitch with the thread you are embroidering.

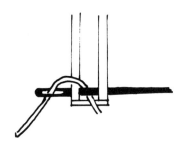

7 ✛ KNOTS AND FLOWERS

French Knot

DESCRIPTION

A full, rounded knot sitting high atop the fabric so that it looks like a little rosette. These are sometimes used in clusters to give a certain kind of textured look that makes me think of strawberries.

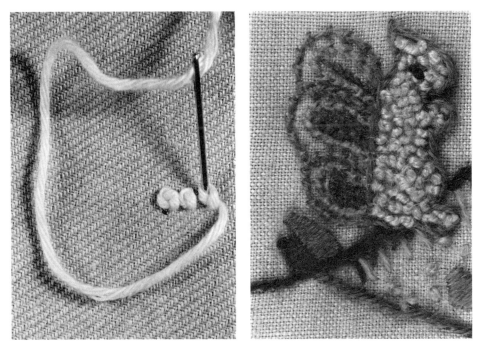

GUIDEMARKS

One dot for each knot you want to embroider.

•

PROCEDURE

1.   Bring the thread up through the center of a dot. Hold the thread
in your right hand and the needle in your left horizontally above the
fabric. Wrap the thread around the needle in a clock-wise direction.

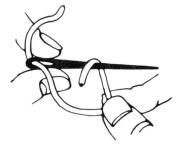

2.   Place the needle point into the fabric to the left of the emerging
thread. Pull the thread tightly against the needle close to the fabric
so there is little space between the thread loop and the fabric.

3.   Pull the thread to tighten it even further around the needle. Hold
the thread and keep the tension while you pull the needle through.

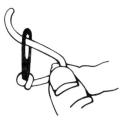

Coral Stitch

DESCRIPTION

A straight thread held to the fabric by a knot placed in the thread at regular intervals.

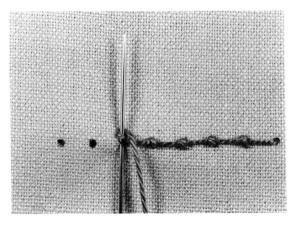

GUIDEMARKS

A horizontal dotted line.
The dots are a quarter inch apart.

• • • • • •

PROCEDURE

1. Bring the thread out at the rightmost dot. Place the needle into the fabric just below the next dot to the left; bring the point out at the top above the same dot.

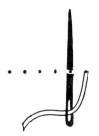

2.   Bring the thread over the needle and under the point, going in a clockwise direction. Hold the thread taut under your right thumb. Pull the needle through. Using the next dot to the left, repeat the directions from step one.

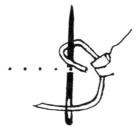

Bullion Knot

DESCRIPTION

A series of loops wound tightly and close together around a central thread and anchored into the fabric at both ends. A cylinder of threads. You can imagine it looks like a silken worm. A hint toward doing this stitch easily and successfully is the needle you use. Do not use a tapered, long-eyed crewel needle; instead use a "round-eyed sharp."

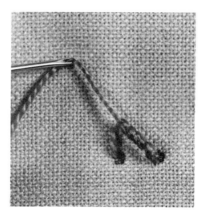

GUIDEMARKS

Two dots a quarter inch apart.

PROCEDURE

1. Bring the needle up at the right dot. Place the needle into the fabric at the left dot, and bring it back out again at the right dot just beneath the thread.

2. Bring the needle about three-quarters of the way through, so that there is a long point around which you can wrap the thread loops.

Hold your right index finger under the fabric behind where the needle comes out. Push so that the needle rises from the fabric.

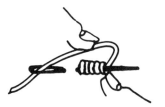

3. With the thread in your left hand wrap it around the needle counterclockwise. Use the thumbnail of your right hand to keep the thread loop close to the needle and next to the fabric.

4. Wrap the thread around the needle four more times, moving your thumb up each time so that it holds the stack of loops close to the fabric.

5.   Maneuver the needle through this stack of loops without destroy-
ing the shape. Push the needle so that it is almost through. With your
left hand grasp the thread; hold it under your last three fingers. With
the thumb and forefinger of that hand hold the stack of loops and the
needle so that it is almost at right angles to the fabric. With your
right hand grasp the needle point and pull the needle through.

6.   Now you have an upright stack of loops and an angled thread
going to the left dot. Pull the long thread to the left to bring the angled
thread through. Place the needle into the fabric at the left dot to the
left of the thread. This will secure the Bullion Knot.

Turkey Stitch

DESCRIPTION

A fluffy carpetlike fuzz of cut theads raised from the fabric. Straight
stitches hold down large loops with a knot at the base of each loop. Rows
of these loops are embroidered very close together. After the area to be
Turkey Stitched has been completed, all the loops are cut to threads of the
same height. This is the same technique used in the making of Scandinavian

Rya rugs. You will need a "loop form" so that all your loops will be the same size. The diameter of the form will determine the height of the loops. Try using a knitting needle or a drinking straw.

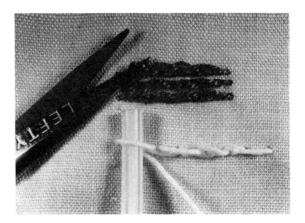

GUIDEMARKS

> Several horizontal rows of dots.
> The rows are an eighth inch apart.
> The dots are an eighth inch apart.

PROCEDURE

1. Bring the thread up at the rightmost dot. Place the needle into the fabric two dots to the left of the thread and out one dot to the right of where you put it in.

With the thread above the needle, pull the needle through.

2. Place the needle in on the same row at the next open left dot. Bring it out just beyond and below the end of the last straight stitch. Put the "loop form" under the loose thread and pull the needle through.

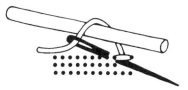

3. Bring the needle over and then under the straight stitch to form a loop around the straight thread. Pull the needle through, tighten the knot around the straight stitch, and remove the "loop form." Continue across the row repeating the stitch. After the last loop, bring the needle up at the end dot above, turn the fabric, and start the next row. When you have finished the entire area of Turkey Stitch take a sharp scissors and shear the tops of the loops so they are all cut off evenly.

Rambler Rose

DESCRIPTION

A circle of stem stitches embroidered close together around a center French Knot. To make the center knot stand out more when making the knot, wrap the thread around the needle twice instead of once.

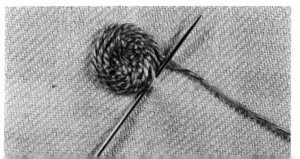

GUIDEMARKS

A circle with a dot in the center.
The diameter of the circle is a half inch.

PROCEDURE

1.   At the center dot embroider a French Knot.

2.   Bring the thread out next to the knot and embroider a row of Stem stitch all around the knot. These stitches should be nearly vertical.

3.   Fill the rest of the circle in with more Stem stitch but from here on they will be horizontal stitches.

Bullion Rose

DESCRIPTION

A series of Bullion Knots worked within a circle. This creates a tight three-dimensional flower.

GUIDEMARKS

A circle of eight dots with a dot in the center. (See directions for Lazy Daisy guide marks).
The diameter of the circle is a half inch.

PROCEDURE

1. Bring the thread up at the bottom of the center dot. Place the needle into the fabric at the lower left, bring it out next to the emerging thread.

2.   Wrap the free thread around the needle as for a Bullion Knot
but only four times. Holding the loops around the needle with your
left hand, use your right hand to pull the needle through. Pull the
thread to the left to tighten the knot; then tack it down at the outer
edge.

3.   Bring the needle up at the center, clockwise, just above the last
stitch. Place it into the fabric to the left of the previous stitch. Wind
the thread around the needle four loops and create the next Bullion
Knot.

4.   Work in a clockwise direction creating Bullion Knots around the
small inner circle. When you complete the circle, embroider one last
Bullion Knot in the center to fill the empty space.

Spider Web

DESCRIPTION

Nine thread spokes crossing each other from opposite sides of a circle. These spokes are then woven over and under with thread until the circle is filled. It is raised and cone shaped, with the spokes raised toward the center.

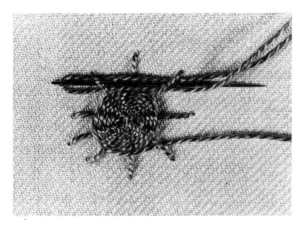

GUIDEMARKS

A circle of eight dots with a diameter of a half inch.

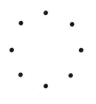

PROCEDURE

1. Bring the thread up at the top center of the circle. Place the point

in directly below at the bottom center and out on the right center edge.
Pull the needle through.

2.   Place the needle in at the center of the left side of the circle and
out just a short distance above at the next dot on the circle's edge.
Cross the circle four times.

3.   Bring the needle out at the edge of the circle, between the first and
last stitch; slide the point under the center crossing threads. Bring
the free thread under the point and pull the needle through.

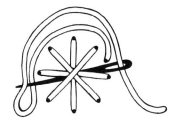

4.   Start weaving, over the first spoke, under the next, and so on until the space is filled.